JOHANN STRAUSS, JR.

concert fantasy for piano, four-hands by GREG ANDERSON

Blue Danube Fantasy
A New Account of the *Blue Danube Waltzes*

for Elizabeth Joy Roe

AWKWARD FERMATA PRESS

Note to performers:

Elizabeth Joy Roe wrote the following in the liner notes to our album, *Anderson & Roe Piano Duo: Reimagine*:

"The kaleidoscopic *Blue Danube Fantasy* takes the elegance of the Viennese waltz as a point of departure and plunges headlong into the passions that undulate beneath the dance's restrained facade."

I couldn't have said it better myself.

Additionally, this concert fantasy for one piano, four hands attempts to illustrate the striking parallels between four feet traversing a dance floor and four hands navigating a piano keyboard. While it may be possible to ease certain technical challenges residing within these pages through redistribution, I kindly request that pianists play the music as it is written; similarly, under no circumstances should the piece ever be played on two pianos. Performing *A New Account of the Blue Danube Waltzes* is the act of dancing, as much as it is the act of making music.

– G.A.

A New Account of the *Blue Danube Waltzes*

for Elizabeth Joy Roe

Concert fantasy for piano, four hands by GREG ANDERSON

Composed by JOHANN STRAUSS, JR.

Lilting waltz ♩. = 60

Piu mosso ♩. = 66

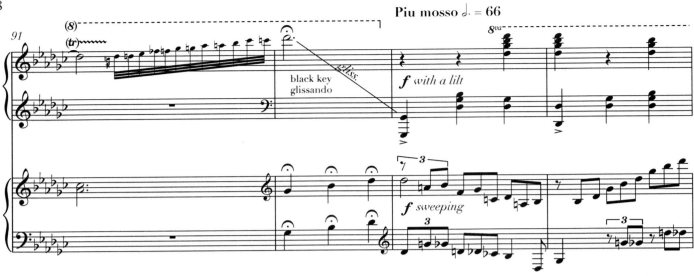

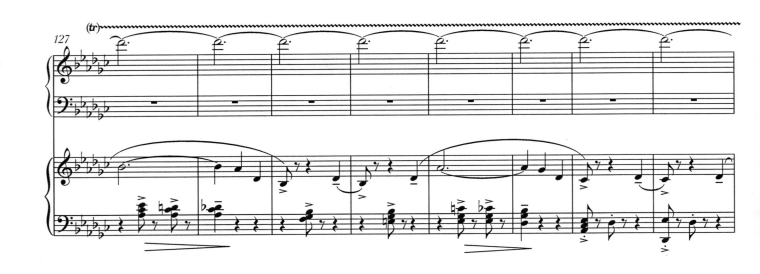

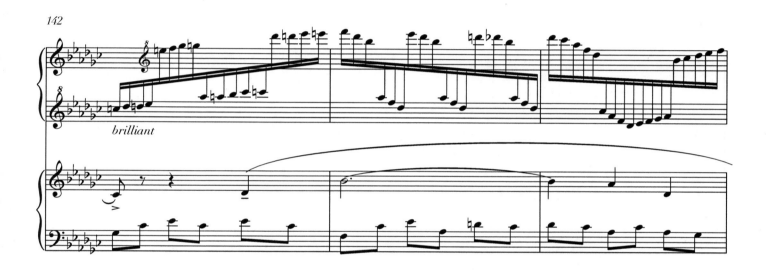

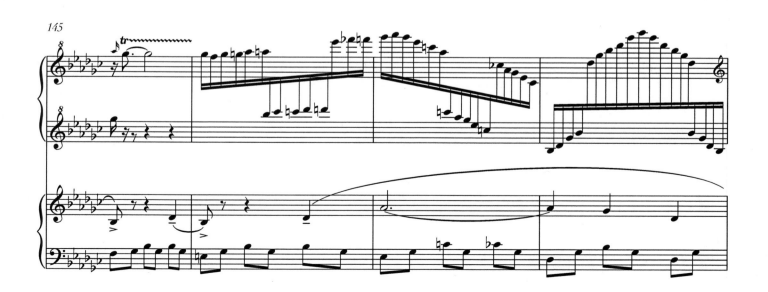

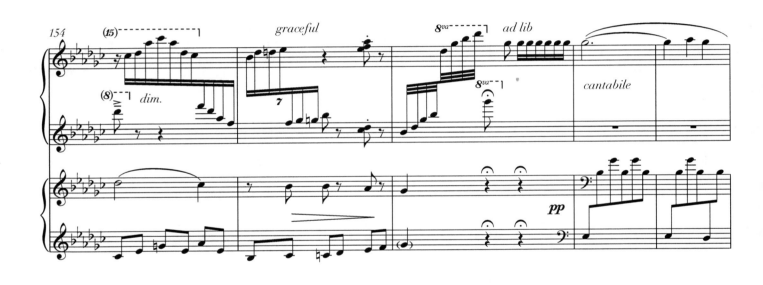

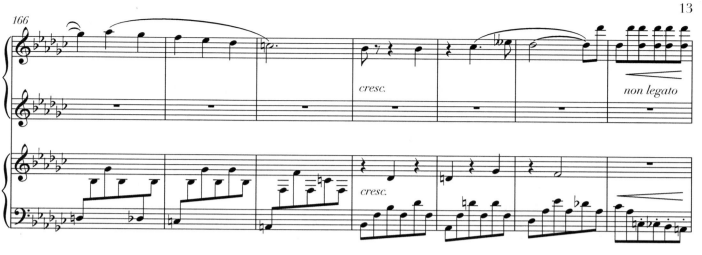

more earnestly

ppp

rit.

poco a poco cresc. et accel.

poco a poco cresc. et accel.

poco a poco cresc.

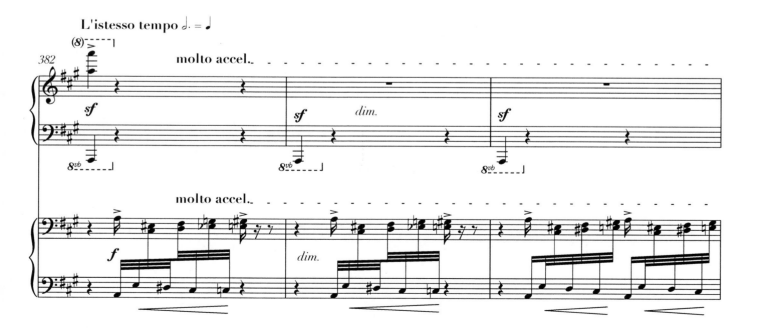

Grand ♩. = 68

Wild and frenzied ♩. = **72**